THE ART OF
KINDNESS

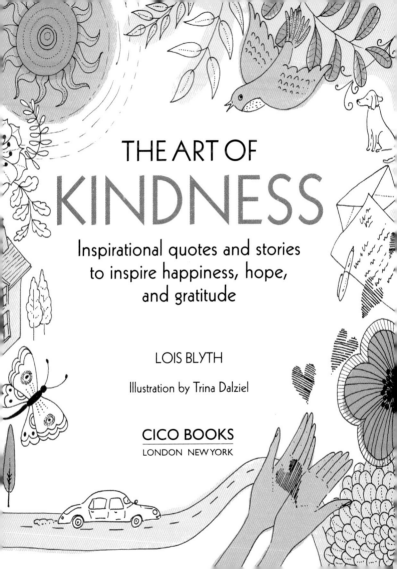

THE ART OF
KINDNESS

Inspirational quotes and stories
to inspire happiness, hope,
and gratitude

LOIS BLYTH

Illustration by Trina Dalziel

CICO BOOKS
LONDON NEW YORK

This edition published in 2022 by CICO Books
An imprint of Ryland Peters & Small Ltd
20–21 Jockey's Fields   341 E 116th St
London WC1R 4BW   New York, NY 10029

www.rylandpeters.com

First published in 2017 as *The Little Pocket Book of Kindness*

10 9 8 7 6 5 4 3 2 1

A CIP catalog record for this book is available from the
Library of Congress and the British Library.

ISBN: 978 1 80065 123 4

Printed in China

Commissioning editor: Kristine Pidkameny
Senior editor: Carmel Edmonds
In-house design/editorial assistant: Kerry Lewis
Senior designer: Emily Breen
Art director: Sally Powell
Production manager: Gordana Simakovic
Publishing manager: Penny Craig
Publisher: Cindy Richards

Contents

What is KINDNESS?

The joy of writing a book on kindness is that it can be based only on personal stories. Kindness is not a place or a thing—although places can have a special niche in our memory, and things may be gifts of kindness. Kindness can exist only when one person chooses to act with heart toward another. It is such a gentle and quiet quality and yet it is the stuff that glues humankind together.

I made some unexpected discoveries while writing this book:

✳ That people find it hard to remember their own acts of kindness. When it feels natural to give, people can no more remember being kind than they remember breathing. It is those who receive the kindness who remember the gift.

✳ That random acts of kindness are often the most memorable—and that the unexpected kindness of a stranger can make us feel blessed and special.

※ That kindness is a feeling rather than an event. Many people associate key life events with memories of people being kind, but may not be able to remember the detail of the kindness.

※ That the most profound experiences of kindness take place when we are at our most vulnerable—when we are in trouble, when we are traveling, or when we are ill or in distress.

※ That sometimes, to receive kindness means taking a risk—the risk of making ourselves vulnerable, letting go of control, or putting our trust in a complete stranger in unfamiliar circumstances.

※ That a kindness can lead to a bond of trust between people that transforms our perception of the world.

※ That the smallest gesture can have the most profound power.

Genuine kindness is a gift indeed. It is offered with good heart, with the receiver rather than the giver in mind. When we nurture our capacity for kindness, we gladden our hearts and take more notice of those around us. But the true magic of kindness is that it has the power to transform the giver more than the receiver, even if the kindness is proffered out of duty rather than good heart.

"Tenderness and kindness are not signs of weakness and despair but manifestations of strength and resolution."

Kahlil Gibran (1883–1931), artist, poet, and writer

This little book is a celebration of kindness in all its forms and recognizes it as the kernel that lies at the heart of other human values, such as compassion, forgiveness, love, friendship, hope, generosity, happiness, and gratitude. There are five chapters that look at all the ways kindness can be seen in the world. **Random Acts of Kindness** explores the power of unexpected acts, both large and small. **Being Kind to Yourself** is equally important—looking after yourself helps you to help others. **Practicing Kindness** is about actively adopting an atittude of kindness. **Giving Thanks** explains how gratitude and kindness go hand in hand. Finally, **Organized Kindness** looks at the bigger picture and where kindness can be found around the world.

If someone has given you this book, the chances are they are acknowledging *your* kindness and the difference that you have made to their world.

Chapter 1

RANDOM ACTS
OF KINDNESS

KINDNESS is Contagious

Kindness is a form of magic. Even the smallest act of kindness can have immense power. A kind gesture can transform a negative into a positive, a warm smile can lead to friendship or create a sense of belonging, a listening ear can offer hope where there was despair. The message that we should "Be kind to our enemies" encourages people to be literally dis-arming. It reminds us that we are all part of the same world. When we are kind to one another, a kind of alchemy takes place. The energy changes. The giver and the receiver feel good about themselves. The recipient of the kindness has a desire to be kind to others also—and so the magic spreads and the energy continues.

"Always, Sir, set a high value on spontaneous kindness. He whose inclination prompts him to cultivate your friendship of his own accord, will love you more than one whom you have been at pains to attach to you."

James Boswell (1740–1795),
diarist, author, and lawyer, from *The Life of Samuel Johnson*

Act of KINDNESS

Putting others before yourself

The KINDNESS of Strangers

Have you ever experienced an unexpected act of kindness from a stranger? At a moment of desperation someone has appeared who has made all the difference, and has then disappeared from your life just as swiftly. Unexpected kindness can feel like a miracle. We are left full of gratitude—but perhaps unable to thank the person directly.

During moments of crisis, it seems we are more likely to experience unexpected generosity of spirit from people motivated solely by a desire to be kind or helpful to someone who is in distress. This may lead us to realize that kindness is an energy exchange. The person you are kind to may not be able to reciprocate directly to you, but the joy of it is they may be more motivated to give, and be kind, to others. It is one of the natural laws.

"No act of kindness, no matter how small, is ever wasted."

Aesop (c. 6th century BCE), Greek slave and storyteller

"The Kindness of Strangers" is a blog that was created in an attempt to fulfill a promise made by a woman called Betsy to a stranger 25 years ago. Spotting her broken-down car on the side of a rural highway in upstate New York, a man, who could have very easily kept on driving, stopped to offer assistance. He spent an entire afternoon helping her to get back on the road, accepting only a thank you in return, and "a promise that I would help someone else along the way." On April 3, 2010, Betsy decided, "It is time I fulfilled that promise. I am making a commitment to be kind to a stranger at least once a day for a year."

And she managed it. Her blog can be read at:
oneyearofkindness.blogspot.com

ICONS OF KINDNESS: Michael Landy

"Acts of Kindness" was a two-month project by artist Michael Landy on the London Underground. He invited us to notice everyday acts of generosity and compassion, however simple and small.

The artist explains, "Sometimes we tend to assume that you have to be superhuman to be kind, rather than just an ordinary person." So, to unsettle that idea, Acts of Kindness caught those little exchanges that were almost too fleeting and mundane to be noticed or remembered.

Landy defines kindness as going beyond yourself to acknowledge someone else's needs and feelings. Being kind to a stranger involves sharing that sense of connection with someone you don't know. "It's a gesture of trust between two people," he says. "There's a risk in that. They may just ignore you or take it the wrong way." It requires courage and acceptance on both sides.

The beauty of kindness is that everyone is capable of it. It costs nothing and it is easy to pass on.

"A hint of fragrance
always clings to
the hand
that gives roses."

Chinese proverb

"Be kind whenever possible. It is always possible."

His Holiness the Dalai Lama (b. 1935)

The Ripple Effect

Kindness has been one of the essential teachings of every spiritual philosophy in the world since time began. It is a survival skill. Kindness has always spread naturally, binding friend to friend and protecting us from our foes.

But only in the electronic age has kindness become a movement. The Internet is alive with good heart and powerful intentions as people around the world find ways to "practice random kindness and senseless acts of beauty."

This wonderful phrase is accredited to Anne Herbert, an American, who is said to have written it on a table mat in a restaurant. Others copied it, bestselling writer Jack Kornfield included her story in his writing, and since then it has spread, literally, around the world, inspiring generous actions and good-hearted gestures in its wake.

"Carry out a random act of kindness, with no expectation of reward, safe in the knowledge that one day someone might do the same for you."

**Princess Diana
(1961–1997)**

"Remember there's no such thing as a small act of kindness. Every act creates a ripple with no logical end."

**Scott Adams (b. 1957),
author and cartoonist**

Pass It On

"Have you had a kindness shown?

Pass it on;

'Twas not given for thee alone,

Pass it on;

Let it travel down the years,

Let it wipe another's tears,

'Til in Heaven the deed appears—

Pass it on."

"Pass It On"
Henry Burton (1840–1930),
Methodist minister

There is a story behind the creation of Henry Burton's verse. A young boy called Mark Guy Pearse was once making the long journey home from boarding school by boat when he discovered that he did not have enough money for the fare. He was extremely anxious and upset and waited in trepidation for the boatman to reach him. Recognizing his honest distress, the boatman reached into his pocket and paid the rest of the fare with his own money. Before Mark could thank him, the man said, "Remember what happened today, and if ever you come across someone else in the same situation, pass this kindness on."

Many years later, Mark Guy Pearse was on a railway platform waiting for a train when he spotted a boy in tears. He asked him what was wrong and the boy sobbed, "I haven't any money left for my fare." Mark Guy reassured him, "Don't cry. I'll buy the ticket for you." As they walked together along the platform, he remembered his promise to the boatman and told the boy to pass this kindness on.

Mark Guy Pearse (1842–1930) was a Methodist preacher from Cornwall, UK. Dr Henry Burton was Mark Guy Pearse's brother-in-law. The story inspired him to write his hymn, "Pass It On."

The KINDNESS of Grandchildren

There are few things in life more likely to melt a grown-up's heart than the sight of a young child rushing up for a hug and a cuddle—especially if that child is your grandchild. A grandchild's hug can make a grandparent feel instantly younger, loved, and loveable.

"My father led a very healthy and independent life well into his nineties; but then he suffered a series of strokes and spent quite a few weeks in hospital and in care. We were terribly worried because he no longer smiled and seemed to have lost the will to live. One day, when we couldn't get childcare, we took our toddler on to the ward with us. Far from being unnerved by the change in her granddad, she rushed up to him, gave him a big squeeze and began to chatter, non-stop. For the first time in ages my father's eyes lit up—and from that day forward he began to make more of an effort to recover. We took Stacey back in to see him as often as possible. There is no doubt in our minds that the healing power of her hugs set him back on the road to recovery."

Jemma

"What sunshine is to flowers, smiles are to humanity."

Joseph Addison (1672–1719), essayist, poet, and dramatist

A SURPRISE PRESENT

"A friend whom I hadn't heard from in years called me for a chat and we were regretting that we lived too far apart to meet up for a cup of tea and a catch-up. A day or so later a mystery parcel arrived at my door. Inside was a special "afternoon tea" package, complete with loose tea, cake, and cookies in a cotton bag. Every time I enjoyed a slice of cake and a "cuppa" over the next few weeks I thought of my friend. My cat adopted the cotton bag as a favorite place to snooze, too."

Tina

HOME-GROWN GIFT

"My parents were great gardeners, and visitors would always leave
with either a posy of flowers or a gift of some home-grown produce,
carefully packaged. I know how carefully those vegetables were
produced, and their friends used to prepare and cook them with equal
care. Somehow food always tastes better, and you feel more gratitude,
when it has been home grown."

Joe

"You give but little when
you give of your
possessions. It is when
you give of yourself that
you truly give."

**Kahlil Gibran (1883–1931),
artist, poet, writer**

Money Makes the World Go Round

Sometimes in life, people encounter financial difficulties. They will often soldier on in private, withdrawing from friends or falling out with loved ones, too proud to ask for help until it is too late. But in some cases, those who care about them will tune in, notice that something is wrong, and come up with a big gesture that makes a life-changing difference:

"Back in the 60s, older friends of my mum and dad gave them the money they needed for the deposit on their first house. Without that help they would not be living where they are today."

Naomi

"One day, completely unexpectedly, I received a check in the post from a client who felt I had done more work than I had invoiced for. Not only was it an incredibly generous thank you, she also funded the first holiday I'd had for a while."

Simon

"My cousin took over the sale of her friend's house and got an extra $70,000 for it! I think this may come under The Most Profitable Act of Kindness!"

Neil

"I run my own business and some years ago had cashflow problems. I was in arrears with my mortgage and other bills, and had reached crisis point. But I didn't feel I could talk to anyone about it. Then my brother came to stay. I was very tense and irritable but he didn't rise to my bad temper. He could tell something was seriously wrong. The morning he left I found an envelope on the kitchen table. Inside was enough money to buy me some time with my repayments and a lovely letter. The money was a godsend—but the letter was of greater value, and I will keep it forever."

Gillian

THINGS WILL BALANCE OUT
IN THE END

"I was vacillating about whether or not to sell my house, but so many things needed fixing and upgrading, and I knew I wouldn't get them done without spending money that I didn't have. In an act of unbelievable generosity, my friend Nicole announced that she wanted to give me her old (by which think 'looks brand new') kitchen cabinets. Not only that, she was going to come and fit them. And there was no stopping her. She put in three days' hard labor and did

"Light tomorrow with today."

Elizabeth Barrett Browning (1806–1861), poet

Act of KINDNESS

Welcoming new neighbors
by taking them a home-baked gift

it to perfection. My new kitchen looked so beautiful, I really didn't want to move! I felt overwhelming gratitude, but I felt incredibly uncomfortable, too. I had received more than I could possibly give in return. How could I ever repay her, or stop feeling beholden? I eventually realized that my feelings were all about me and not about her. I had to believe that, as she said, she really enjoyed being able to help. It helped me to alter my perspective when another friend said to me, 'You know what? Life is long. There will be an opportunity to balance things out in the future.' Nicole assures me that she will not be afraid to ask when that time comes!"

Sarah

Friendship Tokens

A lovely children's story explains the concept of love and friendship. It tells the tale of a village where everyone is happy. The children grow up believing in the idea of friendship tokens. Every time they offer a kindness to someone else, they also give them a friendship token. The more tokens they give away, the more they seem to end up receiving in return, so everyone is happy and everyone has a sense of belonging.

One day, a new child comes to the village, who hasn't got any friendship tokens. She feels miserable and an outsider, and resents the happiness that is going on all around her. She goes out of her way to discourage people from giving away their tokens. "Hang on to your tokens," she whispers. "Don't give them to her; you'll never get as many back in return." Over time, fewer tokens are in circulation and unhappiness and discontent begin to grow. No one really understands why.

One day, an elderly woman, who has seen a great deal of the world, notices that the girl seems discontented, and that every time she starts talking to people, they become unhappy. She gets chatting to the girl and asks her for some help carrying her large bag while they talk. The girl shrugs her shoulders and reluctantly takes the woman's bag.

It feels very light, in spite of the size of the bag. "How very kind you are," the old woman says. "It was so lovely to meet you and spend time with you. I would like to give you some friendship tokens. There are more here than I need. Please take these—and will you come back to see me tomorrow?" She reached into her bag, which was filled with tokens. And the little girl was filled with warmth and suddenly felt good about herself. She began to get a sense of belonging. On her way home she passed a boy who had fallen off his bike. "Let me help you up," she says, "and please have one of my friendship tokens." It just goes to show that the more unhappy and lonely a person appears to be, the more they are in need of the gift of friendship.

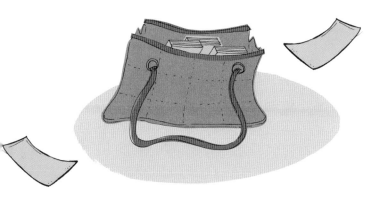

A HELPING HAND

When Vicky moved house, her friend Penny offered to help her pack up and clear the house. On the day, she brought her boyfriend Tim with her, whom Vicky had never met. "One part of me was embarrassed that Tim would be going through our things," remembers Vicky. "But he seemed a nice guy, and I was so desperate for help. My husband was away at the time, and unable to do anything. We had so much to get through, and so little time to do it in. I just had to swallow my pride and accept what was being offered. Tim was absolutely brilliant. He just mucked in and got on with things—and was pretty ruthless about throwing things away, too. I really needed that kind of focus and energy around me. I will never, ever forget such kindness."

"What do we live for, if it is not to make life less difficult for each other?"

George Eliot (1819–1880), novelist and poet

Chapter 2

BEING KIND
TO YOURSELF

You Deserve KINDNESS, Too

Sometimes people forget that they need to befriend themselves.
Until we care for ourselves, and until we are at ease with who we are,
we will not be at peace, and we will not be free to give all of our heart
to others. If we are hard on ourselves, we allow our experiences to
harden our hearts.

"Ask yourself, 'Do I treat myself as well as I would treat a guest in my house?' The answer, sadly, for many of us is 'No.' We are far more generous with others than we are with our own selves."

David Pitonyak, behavioral consultant and writer

Giving to Yourself

We all know people who seem to spend all their time giving to others and being friends to those around them, but who don't make time for themselves. If you are one of them, why not make a pledge to allow time for yourself and your needs. If you can't do it for yourself, do it for those who care about you, because the more you take care of your own sake, the more energy you will have to support the important people in your life.

Book a haircut, decide to spend a weekend away, treat yourself to an afternoon off to read a book, listen to music, or go for a walk. Get the bike out and head for the hills. Whatever you need to do to retune your senses and tune in to your inner self, now is the time to do it.

> "Wherever you go, go with all your heart."

Confucius (551–479 BCE),
teacher and philosopher

Hug, Hug Me Do

If you are on your own, you can still have a great big hug—you can give a hug to yourself. Remember when you were a teenager, imagining that you would be swept away by the love of your life?

Most people have laughed at a friend pretending to have a smoochy hug with someone who is not there. But you don't have to give yourself a smoochy hug. Just wrap your arms around yourself and give your body a big, comfortable squeeze. If you're lying in bed, you can use a pillow for extra cuddle comfort.

It's a great way to start or finish the day and gives your arm muscles a good stretch, too.

"You, yourself, as much as anybody in the entire universe, deserve your love and affection."

Siddhartha Gautama (5th or 6th century BCE), ascetic and sage

Making a Contract with
KINDNESS

You have to be careful with kindness. Being aware of the reason you are giving is important. Sometimes when you give, your intention to be kind may stem more from a sense of duty, or from your need for approval, rather than from a desire to offer a gift of help. And sometimes when you give, people just want more, and that can be difficult, too. If you reach a point where you can only feel good about yourself when you are being kind to others, then you probably need to stop for a while, and start being a little kinder to yourself.

Kindness comes in many guises, including compassion, patience, giving, generosity, friendship, trust, loyalty, gratitude, warmth, and forgiveness.

The more you give of these qualities, the more you will receive in return. But beware of the enemies of kindness: cynicism, doubt, hurt, suspicion, anger, self-interest, and selfishness. The more you give in to these traits, the more upset and hurt you will cause yourself.

"The greatest good you can do for another
is not just to share your riches but to reveal
to him his own."

**Benjamin Disraeli (1804–1881),
British Prime Minister and author**

trust

warmth

compassion

patience

forgiveness

The Power of the Universe

No matter how hard you plan or how well you have prepared, sometimes things just don't go the way you want them to. If volcanic ash grounds planes, or a tsunami hits your business destination, or if the highway is closed because of a fire, there is absolutely nothing that you can do about it. Equally, but in much smaller ways, our best-laid plans are occasionally thwarted through absolutely no fault of our own. Rather than rail against fate, always look to see what new opportunity has arisen because of the unexpected changes. Take the view that there is a reason for it.

Everything that happens gives us a chance to re-evaluate what we are doing, meet new people, or do something else, or even just gives us a break in our day. If you view every event as an opportunity for a new or better experience, you will be less stressed and more open to exciting new possibilities.

"Clouds come floating into my life, no longer to carry rain or usher a storm, but to add color to my sunset sky."

Rabindranath Tagore (1861-1941), poet, writer, and polymath

Look for the Positive

Always looking for the negative in a situation can become a habit that leads to constant disappointment. No matter how bleak things may seem, some form of positive compensation is usually to be found somewhere. Often, a new situation will open another door. We rarely look back with regret at new experiences. Looking for positives tends to make us feel happier, because what we are intent on seeking, we eventually find. Just being positive may help you to react better with other people, which in turn tends to lead to better outcomes.

If you are stuck in a traffic jam or on a train, try to focus on something beautiful that you can see, even if it's just a single flower growing in a built-up environment. Otherwise, mull over what it is the extra time has given you space to think about. Is there something you haven't noticed? The universe has just slowed down so make the most of it!

If you go for a job interview and don't succeed in your application, think about what you learned from the interview. That was someone else's job. Something better for you will come along. Is it time to think about doing something quite different? Did you meet someone else on the way who may lead to another opening or a new friendship?

Developing the belief that there is a reason for everything we experience and for us being wherever we find ourselves encourages us to seek a new perspective. Sometimes we go through very difficult times but what we learn during that period makes us stronger and it may guide us to a happier and more fulfilling life.

"Shortly after I got divorced, I had my heart set on a little house with a garden for me to live in with my two boys. Three times, the sale fell through. A friend told me that it obviously wasn't 'my house' and that something better for me would come along soon. It did, and quite out of the blue. I found a flat that had a door onto a huge communal garden, which gave the boys somewhere much better to play. I have been grateful ever since that I didn't buy the first little house!"

Jane

Smile and Laugh

Have you smiled or laughed at yourself today? What does your mirror tell you? Do you frown or smile at yourself each morning and evening? Smiling makes you feel better. It eases tension and sets you off on the right foot with anyone you are meeting. Smiling at other people often makes them feel better too. Most find it quite hard not to smile back and then you both feel good.

Laughter is also proven to have a beneficial effect on the body and mind. Whether watching your favorite comedy programs, spending time with friends who make you laugh, or reading something funny, make sure you have lots of laughter in your life. Most situations in life have a funny side if you try to find it. Having a really good laugh is one of nature's best medicines!

Helping Others

There's nothing quite like helping someone else to make you understand how blessed you are. Make time to pause and chat to someone elderly to let them know that they are noticed. Help a young parent with a pram; volunteer for a charity or at a local school or project. Even little things mean a lot and somehow helping someone else always makes you feel better and more alive.

KINDNESS is Good for You

It's official. Kindness is good for your health. Scientific research suggests that there is a link between kindness and the hormone oxytocin. The production of oxytocin is triggered by the hypothalamus in the brain. This sends a message to the tiny bean-shaped pituitary gland, which releases the oxytocin into the blood stream so it can do its work.

But where does the hypothalamus get its messages from? And what is oxytocin for? It makes you feel good, and is also known as the "love" hormone, because it is generated by acts of love and touch. Every time we kiss, hug, make love, stroke the dog, or just touch someone's hand, we stimulate oxytocin production and start to feel better about the world. It plays a role in triggering the production of milk in new mothers, and exciting new research suggests it plays an active part in healing heart muscle, too.

Act of KINDNESS

Giving your loved ones a hug

"No longer can we disconnect ourselves from our physical healing ... The way we are feeling might just be the deciding factor in our recovery. And kindness makes us heal faster."

David R. Hamilton PhD, scientist and motivational speaker,
Why Kindness is Good for You

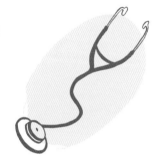

A Hug a Day Keeps the Doctor Away

Hugs are good for our health. They make us feel loved, joyous, and alive.

What is it about human contact that makes it something we can't do without? Experts say we need human contact 10 to 12 times a day. It may be the touch of a hand, a tap on the shoulder, a stroke of the arm, or a hug.

Unfortunately, although humans are inherently social, many will shy away from physical contact, especially if they are feeling sad or lonely. Compared to some other cultures, people in Western society tend to be very aware of personal space, offering a handshake instead of a kiss on the cheek, and keeping a certain distance between each other when engaging in conversation. However, keeping a certain distance is not good for our wellbeing. We depend upon physical contact to make us feel alive and connected to something other than ourselves, and to feel a little less alone in times of need.

Those who have worked in orphanages, or with babies and infants who have been neglected, know that a lack of loving cuddles has a detrimental influence on the physical and mental development of small children. A young child who spends years in institutional care deprived of love and cuddles is likely to become withdrawn, listless, and may suffer weight loss and slow growth.

Hugs especially are so stress-relieving. When we're feeling low, getting a gentle squeeze provides comfort like nothing else—there are even therapeutic practices centered on hugging—but, despite this, many of us tend to turn to other coping mechanisms, such as eating comfort food or crashing out in front of the TV.

So the next time you are feeling stressed, sad, anxious, or just generally downhearted, don't turn for comfort to something that is bad for you—instead, reach out for a hug. When it comes to our health, the best thing we can do is open our arms.

> "I love hugging. I wish I was an octopus, so I could hug ten people at a time."

Drew Barrymore (b. 1975), actor and producer

A Loving Hug is Good for the Heart

A medical study undertaken by a research team at the University of North Carolina studied the effects of hugging on men and women by monitoring 38 couples. Their blood pressure and their levels of cortisol (the stress hormone) and oxytocin (the "cuddle" hormone, a natural stress-buster) were measured both before and after the experiment.

During the experiment, couples relived a happy time in their relationship, watched a romantic movie, talked, and were invited to hug one another.

Both men and women showed an increase in oxytocin levels after the hugs, but for women there were additional stress-reducing effects: their blood pressure went down and their cortisol levels were also reduced.

"We are each of us angels with only one wing, and we can only fly by embracing one another."

Lucretius (c. 99–55 BCE), poet and philosopher

Walking and Nature

No matter where you live, spending time outdoors is one of the most precious things you can do with your time.

Even in the most built-up areas, something wonderful will be growing somewhere. Plants have a regenerative quality. They give us hope. The fact that something is growing stills the mind and relaxes the body.

Try to plan your time so that you venture out of doors every day. Walk in a park and submerge yourself in the beauty of the different seasons. Take a close look at the amazing colors and textures that nature gives us. If you have a garden or yard, love and cherish it. Expensive plants are not necessary to make it beautiful. Wild cornflowers and poppies are stunning, as are bluebells, cow parsley, and rock plants. It doesn't matter where you live, something will grow naturally. If you have no garden or yard, do you have space for a pot or two, or a window box? You can even grow herbs or vegetables. There is little as delicious as something you've grown and nurtured yourself.

"We've got this gift of love, but love is like a precious plant. You can't just accept it and leave it in the cupboard or just think it's going to get on by itself. You've got to keep watering it. You've got to really look after it and nurture it."

John Lennon (1940–1980), musician and songwriter

The Beauty of Trees

Trees play an important role in many cultures and religions. Not only do trees sustain life by providing us with oxygen by day, they also have long associations with myths of fertility, rituals, and immortality.

Who can fail to be moved by the sight of a magnificent tree? They often appear to have faces looking out of their gnarled bark. It is no wonder that different trees and tree types are believed by many to have an energy, as well as healing powers.

Tree-huggers come in all shapes and sizes. They may be small people who want to climb them; animals who hug them while they search for food and habitat; or adults who want to add to, or tap in to, the tree's bountiful energy.

Hugging a tree is simple—just put your arms around its trunk. Offering kindness to a tree is like caring for any living thing: it is all about treating it with respect and care.

The Power of Sound

Wherever you are, you can immerse yourself in your favorite sounds. Ironically, that may mean starting with perfect stillness. If you sit quietly in a comfortable place, at home or out of doors, and just let everything go, you can cherish the sound of birds singing, waves pounding, the wind rustling through the trees, or the rain beating on the window.

You don't even have to be where the waves or the birds are. Plenty of recordings of nature's most beautiful sounds are available, and you can play them anywhere. You can be by a much-loved beach, in an English country garden, or in the depths of Africa or the jungles of the Amazon.

This luxury can be noisy too! Whether it's '60s rock & roll, pop, opera, beautiful voices, choirs, the most up-to-date chart-toppers, or the classics, enjoying the sound of music you love is uplifting and magical. Whether you sit in a comfortable chair with your feet up, lie on the bed, wallow in a perfect bath, or enjoy listening while you're on the move, music is one of life's greatest luxuries and a gift of kindness at the end of a long and tiring day.

Act of KINDNESS

Allowing yourself a moment to stop and listen

Candles and Aromatic Oils

Candles instantly transform a room from mere living space to a place of tranquility. It is not just the aroma that does it, but also the soft light that reflects around the room once the candles are lit.

"I have candles in my sitting room, my bedroom, and my bathroom. In the evening, they are lit wherever I am, as soon as I sit down to eat, read, listen to music, or even watch television. Subconsciously, candles help me to relax and finish my day so that I'm more likely to have a good night's sleep and awake feeling ready for the following day."

Nikki

Candles create a romantic as well as a relaxing environment. Who doesn't want candles on the table for that special dinner? But whether sharing or alone, they make you feel cozy and loved.

Candles are a fabulous gift to give and receive. A gift of a scented candle carries a silent message—relax and pamper yourself.

You can also turn your home into a relaxing haven using aromatic oils. They are readily available and last for ages in a burner, particularly if you buy the waxy ones that melt. Use votives to heat the oil (or they look great in a variety of different containers on their own). You can also create your own scents by mixing aromatherapy oils to suit your mood. Ylang ylang, jasmine, or peony have a sweet scent that can be uplifting, while rosemary will refresh you and lavender will calm you down.

Hand Massage

If you don't have time for a long bath but need to relax before going to bed, try this suggestion for a hand massage from fragrance creator Cath Collins:

"Take a little almond oil and mix it with a few drops of an essential oil that fits your mood. This makes a delicious, soothing treat for your hands. Pour a little into the palm of your hand and smooth into the skin on the back of your other hand; work up each finger individually and massage the cuticles. Do that for each hand. Go back to the palms of your hands, massage each in turn with a thumb, not forgetting the base of your fingers, and then stroke up and over your wrists. It's great to do this just before you turn out the light so that your hands benefit from the oil overnight."

"I began to see that in some way, no matter what subject I had chosen, what country I was in, or what year it was, I had taught endlessly about the same thing: the need for *maitri* (loving kindness toward oneself)."

Pema Chödrön (b. 1936), teacher and Buddhist nun

Offering KINDNESS to Yourself

Many of us are more likely to practice meanness rather than kindness toward ourselves. We judge ourselves remorselessly, making unreasonable demands on ourselves and offering no quarter when we fall short. We would never treat someone we cared about in this way. Offering kindness toward ourselves is an invaluable practice and one that cannot be done too often. People often worry that they feel nothing when doing practices like this, but that is okay. There is no expectation to feel anything in particular, and you should simply continue. Just as a seed grows and puts down roots under the soil long before we see any sign of leaves above ground, so change is happening inside us before we notice any obvious sign of it. If you do this practice regularly, you will notice a difference. This practice is commonly done as a sitting practice.

Sit in a posture in which you feel alert yet relaxed, grounded, and stable. Begin by taking a few moments to connect with the breath. Place your attention wherever in the body you feel the breath most strongly, and just notice the physical sensations of breathing. Remember that the breath is your home base—the place to come back to if at any time things get difficult or you lose your way.

If you would like to, place one hand over the heart. Take a few moments to feel the connection of palm to chest—noticing the sensations of contact, temperature, and movement.

Now, begin repeating two or three phrases such as: "May I be happy. May I be peaceful. May I be well."

Make up phrases that particularly resonate with you. Repeat each phrase silently, noticing any reverberations in terms of thoughts, emotions and sensations felt in the body; noticing any pull of "moving toward," or any resistance or "pushing away." Whatever you notice is simply feedback and an acknowledgment of how things are right now.

Continue for as long as you want to.

Choosing the Bright Side

One powerful way to transform a sense of helplessness is to make a plan to move forward with hope and positivity. We can also choose to focus on other people's needs instead. Offering kindness to others can be a powerful way to redress the balance and change perspective.

Choosing to look on the bright side may sound like a platitude—and may seem difficult to achieve—but the new and brighter moments are usually there, and always worth the hunt. The path to happiness lies in our capacity to see the bigger picture, through positivity, hope, and compassion for others.

Even in the most dire of circumstances it is still possible to choose your attitude to your situation and retain your sense of identity.

"This above all: to thine own self be true."

William Shakespeare (1564–1616), poet and playwright, from *Hamlet*

ICONS OF KINDNESS: The Dalai Lama

Tenzin Gyatso is the 14th Dalai Lama and a Buddhist monk. He was born into a simple farming family and given the name of Lhamo Dondrub before being found at the age of two. Tibetan Buddhists believe him to be a reincarnation of his predecessors and the Buddha of compassion. At the heart of all his teachings is the universal message that we all deserve to be happy, and that showing love and compassion to others is the route to kindness and contentment.

He describes loving-kindness as being the pathway to personal fulfillment. The ability to be kind is part of the life force within us. We need to be kind and show compassion—it is part of who we are. It transcends ignorance, aggression, and attachment, because it is

impossible to be compassionate or kind and also be aggressive at the same time.

But the art of loving-kindness takes practice and self-discipline. If we do not practice it, and show it as often as we can, we may cause harm to ourselves and to others, because we will not be able to overcome our feelings of aggression, and we may not be able to put the essential needs of others before our own.

"This is my simple religion. There is no need for temples; no need for complicated philosophy. Our brain and our heart is our temple. The philosophy is kindness."

His Holiness the Dalai Lama (b. 1935)

Chapter 3

PRACTICING KINDNESS

KINDNESS Opens Doors

Some years ago, a young woman whom I will call Angela was
on a train leaving Waterloo Station in London, England. The whistle
had blown and the train was about to pull away from the station when
she saw a man running, trying to catch it. She threw open
the door and helped him in.

After he had caught his breath and expressed his gratitude,
they got chatting. He was American and it turned out he worked
for a world famous singer, who was at the peak of his popularity.
He was on his way to check out the next concert venue and
to confirm the press schedule.

By the end of the two-hour train journey he had offered
her a job working for the singer. She took unpaid leave from a good
job with a bank to join the tour. As well as having a fantastic time and
loving her job, she had the bonus of meeting famous people,
having a backstage pass at concerts, and being transported in
a chauffeur-driven limousine.

All because she had reacted fast and opened a door
to help someone!

Going Out of Your Way

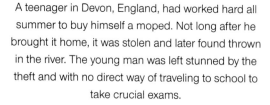

A teenager in Devon, England, had worked hard all summer to buy himself a moped. Not long after he brought it home, it was stolen and later found thrown in the river. The young man was left stunned by the theft and with no direct way of traveling to school to take crucial exams.

But he was even more shocked by what followed. A pensioner, who had read his story in the local paper, came into the café where he worked and gave him the money to buy a new one. She told him she had been moved almost to tears by his story and couldn't believe what had happened, and she wanted to help. But she didn't want any fuss.

The young man was overwhelmed by her generosity and deeply struck by the contrast of how one person could go out of the way to do something so unpleasant while another would go out of the way to put things right.

> "Choose being kind over being right, and you'll be right every time."

Richard Carlson (1961–2006),
psychotherapist and motivational speaker

He bought a new moped with the money and has since got to know his benefactor, who, he says, is a very loving and special person. Her kindness has brought its own benefit—he now keeps in touch with her and has arranged to do some gardening for her, too.

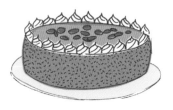

The Spongecake Samaritan

Baking is one of the oldest acts of kindness known to humankind. Somehow cakes, muffins, and cookies baked with heart rise higher, taste sweeter, and look lighter than anything you will buy off the shelf. Many people bake to celebrate, to show welcome, and to express their love for their family and friends. There is nothing like sharing food to bring people together, and nothing like a cake to make an occasion or a person feel special.

Cath Webb, a teacher from Cheshire, England, knows this more than most. She made the national news in the UK with her mission to bake a cake to give away every day for a year—just because she wanted to make people smile. Light, fluffy, and sweetly delicious Victoria sponge cakes were baked daily and given to anyone who deserved a treat, from friends and family, to the local fire brigade, children at her school, nurses, a checkout operator—anyone who was in need of cheering up or had something to celebrate.

It started when a friend was diagnosed with cancer. Words seemed so inadequate that Cath decided to put all her feelings of love, care, and

> "I have never met a person whose greatest need was anything other than real, unconditional love. You can find it in a simple act of kindness toward someone who needs help."

Elisabeth Kübler-Ross (1926–2004), psychiatrist

concern into baking her friend a cake. Her friend was very moved by her gesture—and Cath's mission began. Hundreds of eggs, bags of flour, and enormous quantities of fruit preserves later, she became known as the "spongecake" Samaritan. She kept a diary entry for each of her creations. Each beautifully baked cake was an act of kindness and a tribute to the person she baked for, whisked and blended with love and compassion as part of the filling.

KINDNESS IS STILL KINDNESS, WHATEVER THE MOTIVE

"My boyfriend had been out of work for some time. He was very low and was feeling angry with the world. He is good at carpentry and so I asked him to come with me to help decorate a local shelter for the homeless. He joined me very reluctantly, saying he didn't believe in charity and had better things to do with his time.

Of course, it was a day full of banter and he got chatting to some of the people at the shelter while he worked, who were so grateful to him for putting in a few hours to help out. Receiving such appreciation really lifted his spirits and he offered to come back and share some of his skills. Life suddenly felt full of possibilities again. As he said later, he hadn't realized how much he would get out of helping others. It was hard to know who was being more kind to whom!"

Lucy

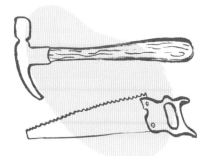

"It is futile to judge a kind deed by its motives. Kindness can become its own motive. We are made kind by being kind."

Eric Hoffer (1902–1983), philosopher

Act of KINDNESS

Phoning someone for a chat (even when you don't really feel like it)

ICONS OF KINDNESS: Mahatma Gandhi

What greater kindness can leaders and politicians bestow upon their people than a personal philosophy based on respect for their fellow man and a political policy based on non-violence? Perhaps the greatest symbol of this ideal is the spiritual and political leader known to generations as Gandhi (1869–1948).

Mohandas "Mahatma" Gandhi is best known for his commitment to peaceful resistance (which he called *satyagraha*, roughly translated as "insistence on truth") and for his leading role in the ending of British rule in India in 1947. Mahatma is a Sanskrit word, meaning "great soul." Gandhi had millions of followers in India and a profound influence around the world even within his lifetime. Not everyone agreed with his approach or his politics. His own life ended violently when he was assassinated by a fellow Hindu on January 30 1948 on his way to a prayer meeting. But that could not destroy the power of his influence.

Many civil rights leaders, including Martin Luther King Jr, were inspired by Gandhi's non-violent approach to protest. He influenced Nelson Mandela. Albert Einstein considered him to be a role model. He has been a symbol of courage for Burmese leader Aung San Suu Kyi. As a symbol of strength and tolerance, Gandhi's influence extends far beyond his time or his country. The power of his words continues to inspire peace and kindness around the world.

"I am mindful that I might not be standing before you today, as President of the United States, had it not been for Gandhi and the message he shared ..."

**Barack Obama in an address to a
Joint Session of the Parliament of India, 2010**

Feel-good KINDNESS

Much of kindness is to do with geography and opportunity. When we tune in to a stranger's distress and realize we can help, it is perhaps an easy matter to take spontaneous action there and then. There is something miraculous about unexpected "feel-good" kindness. It makes the world a better place and those involved will always remember their encounter with a warm glow.

Sometimes, though, kindness is not a momentary choice but rather an ongoing commitment and part of the job description. There are times when it is hard to be kind—times when kindness is mixed with duty or with suffering; and when no matter what we try to give, it doesn't seem to be enough. When kindness becomes a way of life, with generosity of spirit and little reciprocation, it transforms into something else that is bigger than the kindness itself. It becomes love in action and it comes from the heart.

The Gentle Art of Gracious Giving

When someone is in need, it is kinder to be gracious and to ask, "What would you like?" rather than to give that person what you think he or she needs. In that way, the giver offers choice and hope—even to someone whose life feels completely out of control.

Sometimes, sending a short note to say, "I just want you to know I care ..." is all that is needed.

"I expect to pass through this world but once. Any good, therefore, that I can do or any kindness I can show to any fellow creature, let me do it now. Let me not defer or neglect it for I shall not pass this way again."

**Attributed to Stephen Grellet (1773-1855),
Quaker missionary**

The Debt of KINDNESS

Usually in life, it is easier to give than to receive. Being on the receiving end of kindness is not always comfortable. It can be hard to take from others when you are unable to give something in return.

✳ A lot of elderly people know this.

✳ Most people with a disability experience it.

✳ Those who have suffered illness or injury discover it.

✳ Many who have relied on others for practical or financial help will understand it, too.

So sometimes, those we try to help will resent our kindness. They may be unkind in return. In those moments when kindness is rebuffed, or unappreciated, we need to remember that the act of giving is not in itself the gift. Kindness has a greater purpose. It is about caring for our "kind."

The greatest kindness to someone who is vulnerable may be to ask how he or she is feeling, rather than to make assumptions about what that person may want or need.

Making Time for KINDNESS

A lot of us spend our lives in a rush. We email instead of writing letters; we text messages instead of talking; we use voicemail instead of phoning people back. Most of the time that is okay, but it may also mean we have stopped paying proper attention to those around us. Sometimes the greatest act of kindness is giving someone the time to talk, and really *listening* to what they have to say.

"A kind friend is someone who is there for you in your darkest moments; who understands you—and reminds you of who you truly are."

Tanya

"People often say, 'You look lovely; you have a lovely smile; you look great,' and think they are giving you compliments, but those are superficial things. They are very nice to hear, and they hit the surface, but it's all at face value. When someone takes the time to listen to you, that's what really counts."

Bella

"The best way to cheer yourself up is to cheer someone else up."

Mark Twain (1835–1910), writer and lecturer

MONDAY NIGHT IS LASAGNA NIGHT

"A neighbor of mine was diagnosed with cancer, and I knew she was going through a really hard time. I wanted to help, but I didn't want to intrude. So I asked a friend, who had been through something similar, 'What's the nicest thing I could do, since I don't know her very well?'

My friend had a great suggestion: 'Maybe you could offer to make her family a meal once a week. When I was having to undergo treatment, I found mealtimes to be really exhausting, so that would be a good one.'

So I said to my neighbor, 'I really want to help you. If you can think of any way that I can, then please talk to me about it. A friend of mine said it was useful to her to have someone else prepare meals, and I would like to offer you that, if you think it would help you.'

I made a commitment to prepare supper for her family every Monday for six months, and they could tell me what they did and didn't like. But usually it was lasagna, because that was their favorite. So my lasagna became famous, and we became friends, and Monday night became lasagna night!"

Eliza

Offering Words
of Comfort

Get-well letters, or letters to those facing surgery or recovering from an illness, can be difficult to write, but will always be a joy to receive. Aren't affection and caring the best therapies of all? If you are hesitant about putting pen to paper, remember that your letter is a little piece of healing in its own right. Your written expressions of love and concern, tidbits of news or gossip from outside the hospital or sickroom, and your enduring love and best wishes, cannot fail to boost the spirits of the patient. Unsure where to start? These tips may help you to create a letter that will inspire recovery or offer solace.

✳ You might start by detailing your regret that the person has been injured or fallen sick. Was it sudden? You could mention your shock. No matter how formal your relationship is with the sick person, your letter can and should show affection. You can do this by explaining briefly how concerned you are, and letting the person know you are thinking of them. Be respectful of the patient's vulnerable state. Don't dwell on the illness, or your worry, if it is serious; keep the tone positive and bright.

✳ Be careful not to offer advice or to make assumptions. Focussing on recovery may not always be appropriate.

✳ Mention the latest news about the parts of your life you share. You might give them a "newsletter" update of what mutual friends have been up to. Stick to the fun parts of recent activities. You could also tell the person how much they are missed; reiterate that you are looking forward to seeing them up and running, or home again, soon. Mention upcoming events that you hope they might be able to make, but tell them you will provide a full report in case they are still not up to it.

✳ If you wish, take a few lines to express your heartfelt appreciation to the patient for how much they mean to you; point out, for instance, how loyal, funny, and kind they are as a friend, or how great they are to work with, or how much their return is anticipated at family gatherings.

✳ To keep your letter cheerful, you might include light-hearted diversions you think the patient might enjoy. Recount a funny story you saw in the paper (and include the clipping), tell the latest office joke, or offer them a good book or DVD that you think they might enjoy. Perhaps mention new websites or music.

☀ If you feel that you can't produce anything amusing—reasonable enough under the circumstances—you could include an inspiring quote, such as: "Enjoy convalescence. It is the part that makes the illness worthwhile." (George Bernard Shaw, 1856–1950)

☀ As you bring your letter to a close, you may also want to repeat that the person is in your thoughts. Mention mutual friends and acquaintances and pass on their best wishes, too. Finish by offering practical help, if appropriate, and wishing the person a very speedy and comfortable recovery.

☀ "Less is more" when people are seriously ill. Don't feel you have to write a long letter. A carefully chosen card and simple words of warmth will offer enormous comfort.

The Warmth of KINDNESS

Kindness warms the heart and soul. When you do something pleasant for someone else, or when someone does something thoughtful for you, the glow of appreciation is intangible. Kindness costs nothing to give or receive. When you look at another person's life and see a small way in which you can make it just a little better, make that very small effort. It is amazing how good you both feel and how kindness comes back to the giver. Check on an elderly man who is home alone, help someone with the garden, lend your friend something to wear for a special date, or even just open doors for people. Kindness and politeness make your life, and everyone's life around you, better.

BEING TRUE TO YOUR WORD

"It was during the first few days in my village. I had just moved into our cottage, my son was two, and I was on my own--packing boxes everywhere. I was excited, but, of course, anxious about my new life ahead. On about my third day, I was in the courtyard, and a lady passed by. We smiled at each other and had a very quick chat. She said welcome, and asked where I had come from. The next day, when I got back from shopping, a note had been pushed through my door. "Hi, we met yesterday—I know you're on your own with a young child. If you ever need any help, here are my numbers. Please don't feel embarrassed to call; I would be happy

to help." That's it really—she was true to her word and has been a source of support for the last eight years. That small note made such a big impact on me—knowing that someone was there, at my doorstep, and offering their help freely."

Nichola

"The only people with whom you should try to get even are those who have helped you."

Attributed to John E. Southard

The Skill of Empathy

Friends tend to share each other's joy and feel each other's pain; they empathize with one another. The happiness of friends can often lift our own spirits because they want us to share in the moment. Our empathy can also lead us to extend warmth and kindness, and show friendship to others whom we don't yet know.

Empathy is a close friend of compassion. When disaster strikes, empathy and compassion motivate total strangers to help one another. We may not share other people's emotions, but we can relate to how they must be feeling. Empathy and compassion lead to friendships being forged out of the depths of catastrophe or despair.

We are not born with feelings of empathy; it is a skill that we learn through our experiences in early life and as our brain develops. Without it, we find it harder to relate to other people and forge

friendships. It is a vitally important part of being human (although anyone who has had a favorite pet would say that animals can show empathy, too).

"Life is what we make it, always has been, always will be."

Grandma Moses (1860–1961), folk artist

Better Together

Erich Fromm, the German psychologist and social philosopher, and author of *The Art of Loving*, saw the state of loving as beginning with the ability to care for and respect oneself. He saw love not as a separate state in which two people are devoted only to one another and exist in isolation from the rest of humankind, but as an extension of the love we show to one another universally. He believed that in a loving relationship two individuals should be capable of feeling responsibility for each other and showing each other care and respect, taking the time truly to know one another, and they should maintain the ability to show loving kindness to others as well. Such a solid foundation takes time to build, and friendship has an important part to play. We are happiest when our relationships combine both love and friendship, attraction and familiarity, adventure and peace, when we are better together than we are alone.

"Mike is my best friend. He encourages me to be braver and to try new things. And I feel safe enough to have a go because I know he will look out for me."

Stephanie

"I'm a better person when I'm with Steph. She challenges my cynicism and makes me see the good in people."

Mike

Never Be Cruel to Be KIND

Parenting is a difficult job to get right. It is full of apparent contradictions. The advice is endless—and often questionable. "You have to be cruel to be kind sometimes." "You are killing the child with kindness." Can either of these statements ever be true? Is cruelty ever justified? No, never. Can you really kill someone with kindness? It seems unlikely, unless the "kindness" is masquerading as something else—fear perhaps, or anger, or jealousy.

☀ The only rules of kindness are to treat children with love and respect, and to help them to develop the same regard for others.

☀ It is kind to give toddlers clear guidelines for behavior, and to teach them right from wrong.

☀ It is kind to help young children to understand their skills and talents, and to learn to manage their emotions.

☀ It is kind to encourage teenagers to think for themselves, and to give them a safe place to learn from their mistakes, while showing them how to take responsibility for their feelings and their actions.

☀ When our children lose their way, it is also kind to help them to put things right, to regain their self-respect and have faith in the future—but never with cruelty.

"Ignorant kindness may have the effect of cruelty;
but to be angry with it as if it were direct cruelty
would be an ignorant unkindness."

**George Eliot (1819–1880),
novelist and poet**

A Hug is Worth 1000 Words

The wonderful thing about hugs is that when you hug someone, or something, the energy embraces both of you—so it becomes unclear who started the hug or where it will end. You become the hug and the hug becomes you.

Hugs are a short-cut to care and comfort. If someone is distressed, they may not feel like talking. A warm and comforting embrace provides a safe place to cry and to feel cared for—without the need for words.

Hugs can say so much more than words, more quickly, and more warmly. There is very little room for misunderstanding when you are embraced wholeheartedly by someone who wants to communicate with you hug-wise.

*"One joy scatters
a hundred griefs."*

Chinese proverb

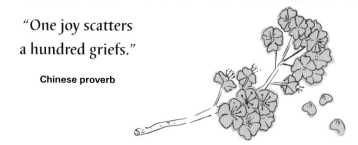

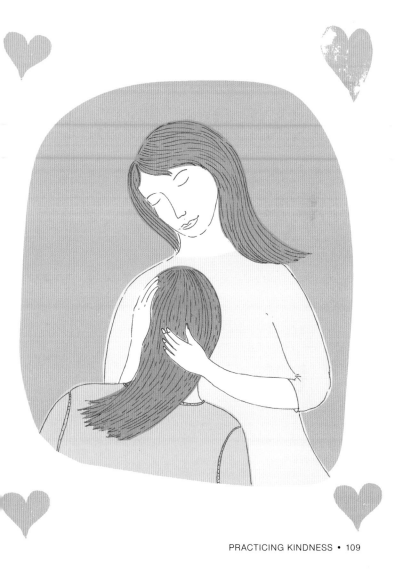

Finding the Right Words

Sending your condolences in writing creates an extremely important, landmark letter—choosing the right words is a task that provides us with the means to permanently commemorate someone we knew or loved, and to give sympathy and healing to those left behind. Close family and friends will read and re-read letters of condolence, and keep them as precious testimonies to their beloved.

For most people, sending a letter of condolence is done rarely, so finding the best ways to express yourself is doubly challenging; indeed, many people don't write at all as they struggle to cope with a bereavement. But expressing yourself can help ease the pain, and since your letter acts as a memorial to honor the deceased, it will have extra value. Keep in mind that your letter should offer comfort to the recipient, rather than unburden your feelings.

As with most important things in life, certain elements of formality should be observed for the letter. It should, ideally, be handwritten on plain, headed paper, although cards and notes are also entirely acceptable.

Your letter does not have to be too long—bear in mind the emotional vulnerability of the recipient, and the fact that the person will probably be dealing with many unwelcome practicalities. But take your time choosing your exact words and phrases; respect your feelings, your memories of the one who has gone, and focus on the comfort you are trying to communicate to the deceased's nearest and dearest. While generally letters are sent around the time of the funeral, many of the bereaved find that the months after a funeral, when all immediate support has stopped, can be a painful time and it is then that a letter is the most welcome.

A GESTURE OF FRIENDSHIP

"My father was one of the kindest people I have ever known. Many years ago the local vicar was briefly arrested as part of a dawn raid by the police. As you can imagine, there was uproar and much speculation and gossip around the village, and the following Sunday at church the congregation was much smaller than usual. My father, who knew the vicar well, as he often read the lesson and helped with events, attended the service as usual. However, when shaking hands with the vicar in the porch on the way out (as is the tradition) he slipped him a bottle of very good red wine that he had brought with him specially and which he had been carefully concealing under his coat. It was a clear gesture of friendship, solidarity, and support at a time when these were in short supply and many stayed away. Kindness personified and a father to be proud of."

Louise

"One can pay back the loan of gold, but one dies forever in debt to those who are kind."

Malayan proverb

"Be kind to each other. It is better to commit faults with gentleness than to work miracles with unkindness."

Mother Teresa (1910–1997)

Chapter 4

GIVING THANKS

The Role of Gratitude

Kindness has a special partner: gratitude. The practice of kindness makes people feel surprisingly good about themselves. It is a habit that is easy to develop. The gift of thanks has the power to transform, also. Offering appreciation is in itself a kindness that can melt the most cynical of hearts. It is so much easier to continue being kind when we feel appreciated. We all know that kindness should be about giving, not receiving; and that the focus should be on others, not ourselves. But it is only human to want to feel valued.

"Never lose a chance of saying a kind word."

William Makepeace Thackeray (1811–1863), writer, from *Vanity Fair*

A Thank-you Hug

A hug is multilingual and multisensory—it bypasses the need for language. Whatever the occasion, there is a hug to fit the bill—even if it is disguised as a handshake, an arm rub, a shoulder squeeze, or the wink of an eye.

A hug to say thank you is a lovely warm gesture that is as wonderful to give as to receive. It tells those who are hugged how much they are loved and appreciated—not only for their gift or kindness, but for all they have offered in love and friendship.

A hug can say, "Hello."

A hug can say, "You're safe."

A hug can say, "I am so happy to see you."

A hug can say, "I'm sorry."

A hug can say, "I love you."

A hug can say, "I'll miss you."

A hug can say, "Goodbye."

Celebratory holidays, such as Christmas, and birthdays are perfect occasions for thank-you hugs. Don't hold back, and make the most of them. But thank-you hugs are great for everyday, too.

Do you have any older people in your life? Do they live alone? Never miss an opportunity to give them a hug, just to thank them for being there and playing a part in your existence.

Put someone you don't know very well at their ease by smiling, and keeping the hug very brief. If it is a "making-up" hug, the opposite applies. Pull the person close and hold them dear, so they understand you are sorry and that they mean the world to you.

Not everyone likes hugging, however, and some people may find physical closeness quite alarming. So when in doubt, don't hug—but always offer the opportunity. Hugs are for everyone who wants them.

Nothing could be simpler than giving (or receiving) a hug—especially if you don't give yourself time to think, and just hug spontaneously. A hug given in love or friendship feels like the most natural thing in the world.

"The shortest distance between two people is a smile."

**Victor Borge (1909–2000),
comedian and musician**

Love, Respect, Acceptance

Love and friendship go hand in hand. We hold great love in our hearts for our dearest friends and will go out of our way for them when they are in trouble or in need of our support. Sometimes just being there is all that is needed to show someone how much we care. Love is about accepting people as they truly are, faults and all, rather than expecting them to be someone else or trying to get them to change. We tend to love our friends because of their imperfections, rather than in spite of them.

Ask a married couple who have been together for decades what has kept them together all these years and they are likely to use words such as "compromise," "respect," "kindness," "acceptance," and "friendship." Ask them whether they love one another and most will answer with an unqualified, "Yes," although they will probably acknowledge that it hasn't been plain sailing and there have been challenges along the way.

"Friendship is the glue that keeps things together when the going gets tough. I must admit, there have been a few times when I have wanted to walk out of the door, and there was also a time when I was very tempted to stray for a moment. But when it came right down to it, he is my best friend. I don't think I could ever do anything that would cause him pain or would hurt him. We have been through too much together."

Claire

"I love you, not only for what you are, but for what I am when I am with you ... perhaps that is what being a friend means after all."

Roy Croft (c. 1905–1980), poet

FIND THE LOVE

"A brief conversation I had many years ago has proven to have lasting positive effects. I was discussing with a work friend a wrangle I was in with a family member. She listened patiently, watching my expressions as well as hearing my words. When I finished, she allowed for a pause and a breath. She looked at me directly and asked, 'Can you find any love in the relationship?' I had to think for a minute, because this question forced me off the self-righteous track I was on. Finally, I took a breath and said, 'Yes. There is love in this relationship.' She said, 'Then go with the love. Just go with the love.' This conversation was like a seed planted in my heart. Every time I recall it and make use of it, it grows. Over time, it has created a habit; to seek out the love element in every situation, especially when I feel ensnared."

Lynn J. Kelly, Buddhist teacher

"What does love look like? It has the hands to help others. It has the feet to hasten to the poor and needy. It has eyes to see misery and want. It has the ears to hear the sighs and sorrows of men. That is what love looks like."

Saint Augustine (d. 354-430)

The Art of the Thank-you Letter

Why are thank-you letters so difficult to write? After a great day out, or the first time you use a wonderful gift, your letter should write itself. But the best of us can struggle to find the right words.

A tradition for centuries, the thank-you letter gives joy to the recipient as barely any other communication does. In some ways, we now live in a world without letters, where texting and emailing have taken over our lives. According to a survey in the early 2000s, a third of people aged under 35 have never written to a loved one. And for everyone today, mail means reminders, bills, or just junk. Yet a handwritten card or letter starts an ordinary day with enjoyment and interest.

While not as formal or as rule-bound as business communications or invitations, it is a common misconception that thank-you letters are the preserve of the older generation. Princess Diana was known—and admired—for her great skill and speed at writing thank-you letters. Internet forums worldwide bear witness to the efforts of mothers to coax their young into the first stumbling attempts to say thank you.

So do we roll with the latest fashions and satisfy ourselves with a quick text or a one-line email, which at least are an acknowledgment? Those of us who write letters know that we all get more pleasure from receiving a "proper" letter in the mail. As a bonus, a thank-you letter lasts forever as a tangible expression of affection.

We know, too, that, as we tell our children, saying thank you is a key life skill—it's a way to value others, and nothing could be more important than that. St Ambrose of Milan, Italy, wrote, "No duty is more urgent than that of returning thanks." And gratitude is good for us—appreciating what we have and are given is a tried-and-tested means to personal happiness. Writing a thank-you letter, choosing the paper, and picking the words focuses your thoughts and strengthens your happy memories of the event or appreciation of a gift; and the finished piece is a small gesture of thanks in return for the joy you have been given.

"Kind words can be short and easy to speak but their echoes are truly endless."

Mother Teresa (1910–1997)

A THANK-YOU CARD THAT LASTS FOR LIFE

"A little girl comes to stay with us sometimes. She is just 9 years old. One day she gave me a little card, and inside it said: 'Whenever you are blue, just know that I am thinking of you.'

There was no particular reason for it. It was just a card that she wanted me to have, so that if ever I did feel sad, I could pick it up and be happy. It really touched my heart.

When someone takes the time to thank you for doing something that to you is just normal, it means a lot, because they are saying, 'You're really special and I thank you for being you'—and that is really kind."

Sarah

"Forget injuries; never forget kindness."

Confucius (551–479 BC), teacher and philosopher

"How far you go in life depends on your being tender with the young, compassionate with the aged, sympathetic with the striving, and tolerant of the weak and strong. Because someday in your life you will have been all of these."

George Washington Carver (c. 1864–1943), scientist

Thankfulness

It doesn't matter how much you have or don't have, there is always something to be thankful for.

☀ If you live alone, be grateful for being able to do just as you please. You can eat what you like, when you like, and where you like, watch what you like on the TV, or listen to whatever music you choose. You can bathe when you like in an uncluttered bathroom!

☀ If you live in a hectic family environment or share with others, be glad for their companionship and the moments you share, for their love, and for the togetherness.

☀ If it is noisy where you are, treasure moments of peace.

☀ If you spend more time alone than you would like, be happy with the peace and find more ways to engage with others.

☀ If you are healthy, the world awaits you in myriad different ways. If you are not, think of ways to improve your health, and don't be a prisoner of your illness. Try not to be a victim of whatever has happened to you and make the most of your life, however long or short it is and in whatever way you can.

"An early-morning walk is a blessing for the whole day."

Henry David Thoreau (1817–1862), writer and philosopher

ICONS OF KINDNESS: Mother Teresa

Agnes Gonxha Bojaxhiu was born in Skopje, Serbia in 1910. Drawn to a religious life from a very early age, she left her home at the age of 18 to join the Sisters of Loreto in Dublin, Ireland. Just two years later, Sister Teresa, as she was known by then, began teaching at a convent school in Kolkata (Calcutta), India. Greatly affected by the extreme poverty that she saw each day, she said she received "a calling within a calling" to leave the confines of the convent and devote her life to caring for the poorest of the poor. With just basic medical training and no funds, she set out to work in the slums. She was 38 years old and completely dependent on volunteers and financial donations. But her reputation grew and her work was recognized and supported.

Two years later, by which time she had been joined by a community of nuns and volunteers, and become known as "Mother" Teresa, she received permission to start her own order, the Missionaries of Charity. They looked after those who were starving, crippled, ill, and destitute, and their work and her reputation grew. A tiny woman wrapped in

a white sari with a blue border, Mother Teresa's face became recognizable around the world. She was a symbol of compassion, love, kindness in action—and a symbol of hope for those in crisis or marginalized by society. In 1979 she was awarded the Nobel Peace Prize. By the time she died in 1997, she had over one million co-workers in over 40 countries around the world. In 2016 Mother Teresa was canonized and became Saint Teresa of Calcutta.

> "You will find Kolkata all over the world
> if you have the eyes to see."

Mother Teresa (1910–1997)

Seeing the Bright Side

Give thanks for your experience of being here in this lifetime. You are here for a reason, whether you recognize it or not.

☀ If you have little money, be thankful for all the wonderful things that nature gives us for free. Make the most of what you have. Share what you have with others in the knowledge that when everyone shares, no-one goes without.

☀ If you are financially secure, be grateful for all you have and be kind to others who have less, but be as grateful for those things that cost you nothing. Wealth on its own makes no one happy, although it certainly helps not to be broke!

☀ Give thanks for every friend, family member, and acquaintance who is in or passing through your life. Every one of them will teach you something you need to know.

☀ Count your blessings. When you feel a bit down, think of everything in your life that is good and for which you are genuinely thankful. Write them down, then bask in the luxury of living.

"Humor is mankind's greatest blessing."

Mark Twain (1835–1910), writer and lecturer

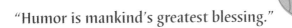

Be More Dog

Dogs take great joy in living in the moment, and being grateful for every adventure. Their appreciation of the everyday is something we can all learn from, whether it's their excitement of going out for a walk, gratitude for their breakfast and dinner, the sheer joy at your return from a short trip out, or the snuggling up to you in the evenings before drifting off to a peaceful sleep after another fun-filled day.

Indeed, there are few creatures more full of joy in life than a puppy wanting a cuddle or a dog that loves its owner, ready for a hug. Dogs give affection unconditionally. Their tails wag, they bark their approval, and they will jump up for more attention (if you let them).

Some dogs are natural huggers. They will stand on their back paws and lean up with front paws at the ready. Others are more likely to think you meant to give them a tummy rub. Dogs and humans have different priorities.

Be careful: never hug someone else's dog before you have been formally introduced. Dogs are territorial and may mistake your intention. But generally speaking a dog hug is warm and forgiving—possibly involving a smelly blast of dog breath and a wet, slobbery lick!

"Happiness is a warm puppy."

Charles M. Schulz (1922–2000), cartoonist

The Nature of Gratitude

Think back through your life—is there anyone who has shown you support and care whom you have forgotten to thank or acknowledge? Is there anyone in your life now who is always there for you, to the point where you take them for granted? When you consider the path that your education and your career have taken, who has helped you along the way?

☀ Say thank you for the small things. Saying thank you, especially for the things we receive as a matter of routine, each and every day, is the easiest and kindest way of making someone feel loved and appreciated.

☀ Do something differently. Memory expert Tony Buzan says that the mind tends to remember things that are different, not things that are the same. So if your routine is unchanged day to day, you will begin to become complacent, because you will no longer notice what you are doing. If you make the effort to do things differently occasionally, or swap responsibilities, or say thank you with a surprise gesture, will stay in the mind for a long time and have a great impact.

☀ Give before you get. We don't need a reason to show people we care about that we appreciate them. Be spontaneous and show someone how much you care before that person has done anything for you.

✳ Walk a mile in another man's shoes. Experiencing the world from another person's perspective is guaranteed to help us to understand that person better. Actions are what create understanding and appreciation.

✳ Learn to accept, wholeheartedly. There is a grace in acceptance and allowing someone else the joy of giving. If you focus on the motive behind the giving rather than the gift itself, you will always know how to say thank you.

"If the only prayer you said in your whole life was 'thank you,' that would suffice."

**Meister Eckhart (1260–1328),
theologian and philosopher**

Chapter 5

ORGANIZED KINDNESS

Danny Wallace's Karma Army

Back in 2002, British comedian Danny Wallace put an advert in a newspaper. It just said, "Join me." All the applicants needed to do was to register and send a passport photo. As Danny says on his website, "No one knew what they were joining. Or who they were joining. Or really, why they were joining. But join they did!"

The problem was, he didn't know why they were joining either! He needed to create a cause.

So he asked people to commit to performing one random act of kindness a week—preferably for a stranger, and on a Friday. The initial gathering grew into a network of people who were motivated to be spontaneously nice just for the sake of being nice. And so Danny Wallace's "Karma Army" and the Good Friday movement were born—a random act of humor turned into something that was pure genius.

Act of KINDNESS

Keep your promises

Danny collected all the stories of kindness and published them in a book called *Join Me*. As he puts it, "It's not a cult, it's a collective!"

The Karma Army still marches on, and has gathered its own momentum around the world. Find out more at www.join-me.co.uk.

"I would rather feel compassion than know the meaning of it."

Accredited to St Thomas Aquinas (c. 1225-1274), theologian, philosopher, and priest

Chain 124

A record-breaking medical chain of kindness took five months to run its course, and spanned America. In the process, Rick Ruzzamenti of Riverside, California, and Donald Terry Jr of Joliet, Illinios, made history. They were the first and last people in a 60-person chain of 30 kidney donors and 30 transplants that was logged by the Kidney Donor Register as Chain 124. It began on August 15 and ended on December 20 2011.

In a medical adventure worthy of a Hollywood epic, Chain 124 was generated by Ruzzamenti's impulsive act of kindness. He simply decided one day that he wanted to donate one of his kidneys and called in to Riverside Community Hospital, to find out how to go about it. His decision set in place a carefully coordinated chain of medical events and procedures that eventually saved 30 lives. Every donation and every operation was an individual story of kindness, benevolence, and love in action.

A longer version of this story was reported by Kevin Sack in the *New York Times* on February 19 2012 as "A string of kindness: 30 kidneys, 60 lives."

"A society grows great
when old men plant
trees in whose shade
they know they shall
never sit."

Greek proverb

EVERYONE NEEDS A SECRET SANTA

"A couple of years ago my husband lost his job. We have two young children, and were struggling financially, but we were able to buy the basics.

One morning I opened the front door to find a large box on the doorstep. Inside it were all kinds of delicious things we wouldn't normally be able to buy, such as olive oil, balsamic vinegar, really nice coffee, chocolates, and cookies. I felt like a child again—incredibly grateful, and intrigued to know who the parcel was from.

Act of KINDNESS

An anonymous act of generosity

It was two weeks before Christmas, and every morning for three mornings, I woke up to find a box of food on the doorstep. By the fourth morning I had started to believe in fairies again, and actually looked for another box! I was pretty certain that I knew who our generous benefactor was, but she didn't want me to know it was her, so we left it a secret.

What we really appreciated more than anything was the care with which she had chosen the contents of the boxes. She had made the giving and receiving so special that instead of being charity, it felt like an exciting treat!

These days we are able to give back to her in quiet ways, but we will never forget that sense of being looked after—and her incredible kindness."

Marie

ICONS OF KINDNESS: Larry Stewart

American philanthropist Larry Stewart (1948–2007) was the original "Secret Santa." He came from a modest background and made his own way in life, earning a substantial fortune from cable television and long-distance communications. But even when he had made a lot of money, he remembered his beginnings, and what it felt like to be out of work. He had especially strong memories of being fired, just before Christmas, two years in a row, when he was in his very early 30s.

The second time it happened, he went to eat at a drive-in restaurant, feeling very down on his luck, and noticed a young woman washing cars outside. It was a bitterly cold day and she was wearing a very light jacket. The story goes that the sight of her working so hard for "nickels and dimes" made him reflect on his own situation and realize that things could be worse. When she washed his car, he gave her a $20 tip and she burst into tears of gratitude. That small sum had made a significant difference to her life.

From that time on, until a year before his death, he used to give away small amounts of cash, anonymously, and often in $100 bills, to those in need. The total amount he gave away is estimated to be $1.3 million. He also donated to community charities, but had great belief in giving spontaneously and directly to people who needed it, so that they did not have to ask anyone for help.

In his mid-50s Larry was diagnosed with cancer and began "training" other people to be Secret Santas before the due holiday season. Sadly, he died a year later, but the tradition still lives on. Since then, Larry Stewart's humble generosity has inspired a whole movement.

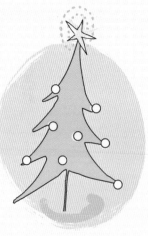

Cards and Letters

There is something quietly exciting about hearing the dull thud of a greetings card landing on the doormat, or receiving a handwritten envelope in the mail. Those of us of a certain age are probably still likely to send a card or a letter if we want to say something important or a lasting thank you, although letter-writing in the sense of keeping up a correspondence is probably a dying art. Some old-fashioned ways to make sure your friends feel cared for:

✴ Remember birthdays. Don't just phone, send a birthday card that can be savored, displayed, and treasured.

✴ Send postcards. You don't need to go on vacation to send a postcard. It's fun to send them with a short note, day to day.

✴ Write a "real" letter. Why not take the time to send a handwritten note to a relative or a friend? It is as much of a keepsake as a gift, and possibly more precious.

Friendship and Kinship

True friendship is about so much more than "you and me." It is about mutual support and human survival. As any soldier on the battlefield knows, a friend is someone who covers your back when you are facing grave danger. Friends stand together to face a common enemy, and would never leave one of their own kind to perish unaided.

Away from the battlefield, silent enemies can be equally life-threatening. Loneliness and isolation steal many lives. Feeling unsupported and unloved takes a toll on the body as well as the mind. Reaching out in friendship to those who seem alone, neglected, or in need is as necessary as breathing. If we turn our backs on those who need companionship the most, we turn our backs on our own humanity and the compassionate future of our own kind.

We are only as wealthy as the poorest among us, and we are only as kind as those in need allow us to be.

"Every winter for the last five years or so, an elderly man has returned to our small market town. It is impossible to tell exactly how old he is, but he is clearly living rough, and moves from place to place during the year. Last year we were especially concerned about him as the winter forecast was severe, so a local builder converted the annexe at the rear of our local church into a small flat. It included a kettle and a stove, a bed and a shower. We invited him to move in. He was quietly grateful, and stayed for two nights. By night three he was on the move again, perhaps feeling constrained by his new existence. Some people felt affronted, but he didn't mean to offend anyone! I'd like to hope he will be back again this year, knowing that he has a safe and warm place to stay should he need it."

John

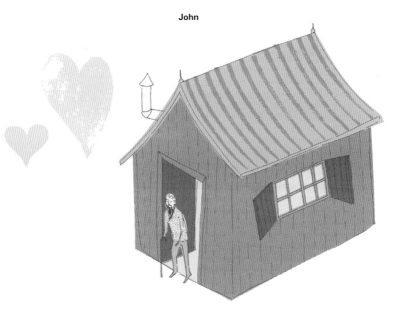

National Friendship Day

In 1935, the United States Congress proclaimed the first Sunday in August National Friendship Day. The year-round exchange of friendship cards picked up in the late 1950s and rapidly gained in popularity during the '60s and '70s and remains popular today.

Taking a moment to send a card, or a text message or an email, to say hello, or "I am thinking of you," will always have the power to make someone else's day.

"Do all the good you can,

By all the means you can,

In all the ways you can,

In all the places you can,

At all the times you can,

To all the people you can,

As long as ever you can."

**John Wesley (1703–1791),
founder of Methodism**

Charity and Fundraising
Thank-you Letters

To thank charitable donors personally is vital to the success of any community organization, yet somehow the task can fall by the wayside. Thanks as well as appreciation are essential—your givers will want to know how their donations are being spent. And, as a way to maintain the interest of committed and regular donors, your letter can also become a valuable marketing tool. Several "giving" surveys reveal that the speed of response to a gift increases the chances of getting further, larger donations in the future. It makes good sense. Everyone like to feel appreciated.

Keep your thank-you letter professional—use a letterhead, and do not plaster your letter with logos or bright colors. Your letter should reinforce the credibility of your cause. You should send it from the most senior person in your organization, or the Head of Donations. Similarly, address your letter to the most senior person involved in the giving; for example, if you are thanking a school, address it to the head teacher or principal. Make it personal—a typewritten letter is fine, but avoid obvious photocopies, and, if you can, handwrite the salutation and sign it in ink.

Unlike a social thank-you letter, include a specific mention of the sum; this also acts as a receipt for tax. Then, if your donor has given time and effort, list the tasks he or she did to help. Remember that your donors are your partners in a shared endeavor—treat them as such with plenty of information about how the community organization is doing as a whole.

You should explain how your organization has benefited from their help. Say what their donations achieved, in detail. Make your description as tangible, and lively, as possible. Include case studies if you can—for instance, the gift of a water pump to an African village could be illustrated with stories about the village's healthy and happy mothers and children.

Experts recommend that it is wise to time the letter for the end of the financial year, if possible, and to point out any tax breaks your donors may get, or can apply for, on behalf of themselves or your organization. However, save campaigning, or asking for more help, until you next get in touch—this letter is purely a courtesy.

"It is the greatest of all mistakes to do nothing because you can only do a little. Do what you can."

Sydney Smith (1771–1845), writer, wit, and cleric

Friendship Dolls

In 1927, Dr Sidney Gulick of the Committee of World Friendship among Children, arranged for 12,739 blue-eyed American friendship dolls to be sent to Japanese children, as a gesture of goodwill and to encourage international understanding and friendship. In exchange, 58 beautifully produced and individually unique dolls, dressed in kimonos, were sent from Japan to libraries and museums across the USA. Parties were thrown for the dolls and they were transported miles around the world as goodwill ambassadors for both countries.

The Secret of Enthusiasm

Benjamin Zander is a world-renowned conductor, teacher, and author of an inspirational book, *The Art of Possibility*. He holds an unshakeable belief that 100 percent of the world's population can be encouraged to love classical music, and his enthusiasm makes it easy for others to be caught up in his excitement for his subject. He makes people laugh and feel happy as they listen to him, and because he leads, they are happy to follow. His passion enriches lives.

In his memorable talk at a TED conference in 2008 (these are annual conferences devoted to ideas and creativity in the fields of technology, education, and design), Zander spoke of his realization that "the role of the conductor is not to make a sound, but to awaken the art of the possible in other people." And that is the power of enthusiasm. When someone cares so much about something, it is easy for others to feel that energy and be invigorated by it.

Benjamin Zander's litmus test to tell that he has brought the crowd with him, is to look in people's eyes. As he says, if their eyes are not shining, he has to question what he needs to do differently.

His words are inspiring because his is a philosophy that could bring happiness to the whole world. What if, instead of focusing so much on our own happiness, we focused on making others' happiness possible? What if, instead of aiming small and wanting one or two people to be happy, we all aimed big and worked to make the whole world happy? Could this work? How can it happen?

In order to have an impact, we need to focus on influencing those around us; they will then go on to influence the people they know, and so the ripple effect continues.

"Who are we being, that our children's eyes are not shining?"

Benjamin Zander (b. 1939), musician

Spiritual Awareness

Many people lose their sense of happiness because they come to believe their life has no meaning. There are as many reasons for this as there are people on the planet. To paraphrase Tolstoy, every lost person becomes lost in their own way.

For many, this sense of loss stems from an absence of spiritual influence in their lives. We are spiritual as well as physical beings, and can communicate by using our senses and mind—but in order to do so, we need to become aware of, and be back in tune with, our soul.

Scientists such as Martin Seligman, who have devoted their professional lives to understanding the nature of happiness, focus more on the mind than on the notion of soul, but they have discovered that those who succeed in living a purposeful life are the happiest.

A purposeful life tends to mean one that is focused on a goal or a mission that is greater than the needs of the individual alone. Altruism and selflessness enhance the chosen path. Great spiritual leaders, such as Mother Teresa, the Dalai Lama, and Archbishop Desmond Tutu, and secular leaders, such as Nelson Mandela, Gandhi, and Aung San Suu Kyi, all display a calm hinterland and a sense of purpose that give them a spiritual quality. They are acting for the greater good; the quest to improve the wellbeing of others has overtaken any inclination to focus solely on their own needs.

For many, spiritual awareness involves a ritual of worship. Prayers, chants, hymns, and offerings of thanks play an important role in every doctrine. The vibration, rhythm, and symbolism of each stage of the process have a profound effect on the human mind and body. These ancient ways make the body resonate, literally, with the power of the words and music. Those with greater understanding explain that it is by resonating at a higher level that it is possible to become in tune with the Divine.

Those who seek spiritual awareness are seekers after the ultimate truths in life; they are willing to give themselves over to a higher power and to have faith in life's greater purpose. Many on the path to spiritual happiness are searching for a state of bliss. Ironically, differences in spiritual doctrine and rigid adherence to the rules of religious dogma

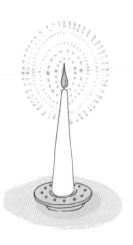

have been at the heart of wars, church schisms, civil unrest, and various societies' prejudice for centuries. We seem no closer to universal peace and understanding now than at the time when religion began.

However, for the awakened soul, spirituality transcends dogma. Spirituality has little to do with the differences in the way we worship, and has everything to do with those aspects of our natures that are universal and that, at best, make human beings a force for good, and happiness epitomized. Those who succeed in living a purposeful life are the happiest.

"To one who has faith, no explanation is necessary; to one without faith, no explanation is possible."

St Thomas Aquinas (c. 1225–1274), theologian, philosopher, and priest

Awakening to Spiritual Happiness

There are many and varied paths leading to spiritual awareness and everyone has to find their own way to meaning. Each religious tradition has its own set of belief systems and rituals, although at the heart of each doctrine the principles and basic practice are fundamentally the same:

❋ Belief in a higher power

❋ Faith

❋ Time devoted to learning about spiritual matters

❋ A general belief in our need to love one another as fellow human beings and to strive for a fairer and better world

❋ A ritual of prayer and devotion that has the power to make people feel closer to their higher power and stronger within themselves

❋ A call for a simple life, free of possessions and the trappings of materialism

❋ The teaching that we should love others more than ourselves

Do we need to give up everything and devote our lives to prayer in order to develop spiritual awareness? That question is set to run and run. There is simplicity and freedom in having nothing, which those who have spent time traveling the globe understand well. When we have few or no possessions, we become truly equal. Envy and dissatisfaction disappear. We become more connected to mankind.

But something more than that is at work. Spiritual awareness for most people means acknowledging something greater than ourselves—a force of love that encourages us to be humble and put the needs of our own ego to one side for others and the common good.

Every so often we are privileged to meet someone who seems to shine with an inner glow, whose kindness and selflessness come not only from the heart, but from a place inside that seems to connect with the greater good and needs of humanity. These are the people who always care about others; whose words of wisdom have a way of soothing trouble and lifting people's spirits; whose faith in something other than themselves seems to fill them with strength in adversity. They have discovered the power of happiness in the art of spiritual awareness.

Spiritual awareness develops in stillness:

pause

breathe   **look**

listen

Being Kind

One secret of happiness is more effective and more vital to well-being than any other, and that is to be kind to others—not just when you feel like it, or because today is world kindness or happiness day, or because you want to feel good about yourself but because being kind to others is the only true way for us to find happiness in this world.

In the spirit of "Imagine," John Lennon's song of universal love and hope, imagine what it would be like if everyone was kind, all the time. We are not talking about the home-baked and sugary kind that overindulges and makes us feel slightly queasy. We are talking about habitual kindness; hard-to-give kindness; being kind before you have received kindness; being kind because it is simply the right thing to do; being kind even if you have a sense of dislike for someone; loving kindness and forgiving kindness.

Kindness lies at the heart of happiness because when we help other people, we feel good about ourselves. Kindness is also an energy for good; those who receive kindness are more likely to give kindness.

*"Love conquers all things:
let us, too, give in to love."*

Virgil (70–19 BCE)

The Art of Giving

There is a secret to giving that not everyone has discovered but which is a source of optimism for the world. The good news is that giving to others is good for you. It will make you happy. It will make you feel better about yourself.

I spoke recently to someone whose mother had moved to a smaller home. They sorted through all her possessions and deciding what to let go had been painful for both of them, even donating books and goods to a thrift store had proved hard. But the charity they chose runs a scheme whereby donors are sent an update on how much money their items have raised. Receiving these letters made my friend's mother so happy that over time she began to give away even more.

In 2010, the Charities Aid Foundation (CAF) joined with *The Sunday Times* to ask 69 of the UK's wealthiest people about the reasons for  their philanthropy. The majority said the main reason was that they enjoyed giving. Over half wanted to leave a positive legacy. In the United States, Bill Gates is leading the way via the Bill and Melinda Gates Foundation. He has personally donated millions of dollars, and, with Warren Buffett, has launched "The Giving Pledge," inviting billionaires to make a moral pledge to leave at least 50 percent of their fortunes as a legacy to philanthropic causes. Media mogul Simon Cowell has been quoted in the past as crediting Oprah Winfrey for helping him to discover how good it makes you feel to give money away as well as make it.

But giving isn't just about money. The most valuable gift of all is your time—time spent in the service of others, listening and paying attention. The concept of service may seem old fashioned in the modern world, but the nature of service goes much deeper than the odd good deed. When we are able to serve others, modestly, but putting the needs of the ego to one side, we become more humble, less focused on self, and more aware of the strengths of those around us.

Loving KINDNESS

When we are young children, our own needs are all-consuming. Our focus is on our own comfort and survival; all else is secondary. As we grow older and our minds open and develop, we come to understand that the needs of other people are as important as our own. With this realization comes the richness of appreciating other people and being appreciated ourselves; friendships grow; sacrifices are made for the greater good of a situation, and we discover that taking care of other people's needs reaps its own rewards. We feel loved, connected, of value, and appreciated; and it can make us feel good about ourselves, too. Happiness grows with loving kindness.

The concept of loving-kindness lies at the heart of all faiths around the world. It focuses on paying loving attention to the needs of others—and loving them as ourselves. Loving-kindness is not about selfless martyrdom but encourages us to use wise discernment in deciding how to act in any situation—with empathy, compassion, forgiveness, love, and understanding. In Buddhism it is known as *metta*, in Sanskrit it is *maitri*. The Dalai Lama talks and writes about the steps toward loving kindness that are central to learning to follow a spiritual path.

Each of us has the capacity for loving kindness, but sometimes it is consciously suppressed, due to an event that has happened in our lives. Perhaps a difficult decision taken at work has caused someone pain or hardship; perhaps a choice made in our personal life has had a negative impact on others; perhaps something so painful or hurtful has happened that we can't bear to look at it too closely. When life is tough, we toughen up to get through. Sometimes the walls of self-protection remain in place to prevent us from looking too closely at what has happened.

"Love is that condition in which the happiness of another person is essential to your own."

Robert A. Heinlein (1907–1988), science fiction author

Being Kind

One secret of happiness is more effective and more vital to well-being than any other, and that is to be kind to others—not just when you feel like it, or because today is world kindness or happiness day, or because you want to feel good about yourself but because being kind to others is the only true way for us to find happiness in this world.

In the spirit of "Imagine," John Lennon's song of universal love and hope, imagine what it would be like if everyone was kind, all the time. We are not talking about the home-baked and sugary kind that overindulges and makes us feel slightly queasy. We are talking about habitual kindness; hard-to-give kindness; being kind before you have received kindness; being kind because it is simply the right thing to do; being kind even if you have a sense of dislike for someone; loving kindness and forgiving kindness.

Kindness lies at the heart of happiness because when we help other people, we feel good about ourselves. Kindness is also an energy for good; those who receive kindness are more likely to give kindness.

"Love conquers all things:
let us, too, give in to love."

Virgil (70–19 BCE)

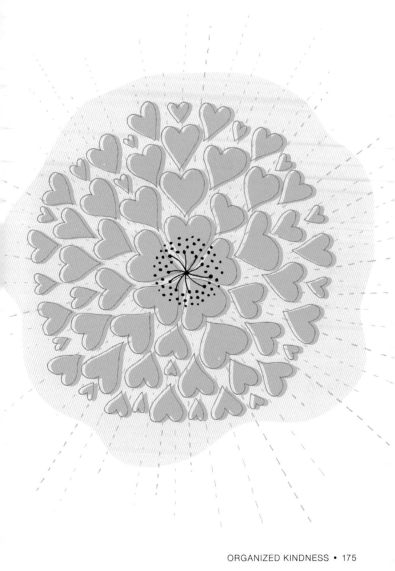

Acknowledgments

The publishers are grateful for permission to reproduce extracts from works in copyright.

Page 16: Michael Landy's Art of Kindness project is online at http://art.tfl.gov.uk/archive/actsofkindness/sendstory.

Page 37: Quotation © David Pitonyak from "The importance of belonging: a report on men and friendship in the 21st century" (Chivas Regal, 2012).

Pages 78–79: This story was first reported in *The Sidmouth Herald*.

Page 124: Quotation © Lynn Kelly from "The Buddha's advice to lay people" (www.buddhasadvice.wordpress.com). Reproduced with permission.

Every effort has been made to contact copyright holders and acknowledge sources, but the publishers would be glad to hear of any omissions.

About the Author

Lois Blyth was a writer of self-help and lifestyle books, including *The Little Pocket Book of Happiness*, *The Power of Gratitude*, and *A Year of Living Thankfully*.